THE HENRY L. STIMSON LECTURES   YALE UNIVERSITY, 1971

NEW HAVEN AND LONDON, YALE UNIVERSITY PRESS, 1972

AFTERNOON

ON THE

POTOMAC?

A BRITISH VIEW OF AMERICA'S

CHANGING POSITION IN THE WORLD

BY ROY JENKINS

© 1972 by Roy Jenkins
All rights reserved. This book may not be
reproduced, in whole or in part, in any form
(except by reviewers for the public press),
without written permission from the publishers.
Library of Congress catalog card number: 77-188329
International standard book number: 0-300-01586-0

Designed by Sally Sullivan
and set in Linotype Times Roman type.
Printed in the United States of America by
The Colonial Press Inc., Clinton, Massachusetts.

Published in Great Britain, Europe, and Africa by
Yale University Press, Ltd., London.
Distributed in Canada by McGill-Queen's University Press, Montreal;
in Latin America by Kaiman & Polon, Inc., New York City;
in India by UBS Publishers' Distributors Pvt., Ltd., Delhi;
in Japan by John Weatherhill, Inc., Tokyo.

CONTENTS

1 The United States and the World:
  1917–1963   1

2 Britain's Changing Perspective: 1945–1971 21

3 The Future International Role of the
  United States   41

1 THE UNITED STATES AND THE WORLD: 1917–1963

One of the most surprising features of world history in this century was the entry of the United States into the European War in 1917. The pressures were so much less compelling than in 1941. It was surprising for a whole variety of reasons. It was a European and not a world war. America was only marginally emerging as a great power of the first order. The acts of maritime provocation in the Atlantic were fairly minor. The German influence in the United States was strong and recent. Britain and France would not necessarily have lost without America. It was a peculiarly disagreeable war in which to participate. And the menace of kaiserism was of an altogether different and lesser order than that of nazism.

Yet it all then happened with a curious ease. Britain and France were of course much relieved that it did. But it was a great contrast with the unsteady and tantalising evolution, against a background of European catastrophe, of American involvement in 1939–41. Woodrow Wilson's interventionist determination, after 1916, was much stronger than that of Franklin Roosevelt. I am a greater admirer of Roosevelt than of Wilson, but I find an odd contrast between the actions of the one in 1917 and the other in early 1941, even after the third term was settled, when there might easily have been no European democracy left to save in "God's good time."

No doubt the relative precipitateness of the earlier period produced its own reaction in 1919–21. Europe then settled down to making a mess of its own affairs.

America settled down to normalcy, weak government in Washington, business dominance, and the boom years.

The Atlantic was very wide indeed during the twenties. This was true in all senses. It was true in the most literal sense that it still took a long time to get across. Apart from Lindbergh and a very few others, nobody did it in less than five days. Very few, except those who were both rich and under-occupied, did it at all frequently. The overwhelming majority, including leading politicians on both sides of the ocean, never crossed it at all. As a result, the world of the speakeasies, of Al Capone, and indeed of Al Smith was very remote from London or Paris. The movies in a sense accentuated rather than bridged the remoteness. The world they portrayed to us was as vivid but unreal as a Verdi opera. Scott Fitzgerald was something of a bridge, but his whole approach to Americans in Europe, with its sense of breathless excitement about their being there at all, showed how wide the span had to be.

Washington seemed even more remote than New York. By present-day standards the activities and influence of the federal capital were indeed fairly remote from the lives of most Americans. Still more were they remote to Europeans. It is a platitude to say that the politics of the Harding-Coolidge era were inward-looking. The Hoover administration—as I should say even if I were not delivering a lecture on the foundation of its Secretary of State—were a good deal less so. And indeed by then the slump was undermining the American complacency of the middle twenties and making the two sides of the Atlantic more conscious of their ability at least to infect each other. The slump also produced the presidency of Franklin D. Roosevelt, which, as it turned out, was the decisive stage in the evolution of the United States to full world power, and of Washington, despite a certain lack of metropolitan advantage, to a position as near to the political capital of the world as has ever been occupied by any city since the fall of imperial Rome.

I use the phrase "as it turned out" partly because this is in general a suitable phrase to use about the march of events under the Roosevelt régime. A great deal was done, but not very frequently in accordance with a clearly announced prior plan. And I use it also because it was far from clear in the early days that the Roosevelt presidency was going to turn the United States in an internationalist direction. The 1932 campaign was as domestic as any that has ever been fought. The first inaugural contained plenty of vision for America but little for the world. And the new President's first effective intervention on the international scene, when he broke up the 1933 World Economic Conference rather than agree to a system of mutually agreed currency parities, may have been good sense for the dollar and the United States economy but was certainly not signally cooperative. Beyond the unsuccessful attempt in 1935 to secure United States adherence to the World Court, and the Tripartite Pact of 1936, it is difficult to think of any notable internationalist action taken by Roosevelt during his first term.

Thereafter events to some extent took charge. Europe gyrated round a whole series of hairpin bends on the long, sickening descent towards war. The downward pressure from the dictators was relentless. Britain and France lacked the will or the ability to stand against the process. They just skidded round the corners and stayed on the road, until by the summer of 1939 there was no further room for such manoeuvres. During these years the United States administration observed what was happening with a mixture of dismay, apprehension, contempt for the weakness of the British and French governments, and short-term relief that it could hardly be expected to run risks for those who would not stand and fight for themselves. There were substantial bodies of opinion in Western Europe who were opposed to the policies of their governments and wanted an end to appeasement. Although by no means exclusively so (Churchill, of course, being the outstanding example the other way) these groups tended to be on the left-centre in politics. They were disillusioned not only with supineness before Hitler and Mussolini but also with supineness when faced with unemployment and poverty at home. On both counts Neville Chamberlain, Prime Minister of Britain from 1937 to 1940, was their antihero. It was necessary but more difficult to find a hero. There was none available on the left in Britain. Churchill was too right-wing, Lloyd George too old and unreliable, Attlee too colourless, Stafford Cripps too disruptive. Léon Blum in France momentarily looked a better candidate, but although personally brave and intellectually distinguished, he lacked buoyancy and survival power.

Roosevelt manifestly lacked neither of these qualities, and so, to some extent filling a gap, he began to achieve a hero's role for the moderate left: and not always only for the *moderate* left, as in the case of John Strachey, who swung in two years from a fully cataclysmic Marxist position to intense admiration of the later stages of the New Deal. In part this turning of European eyes westward was based on a simple desire for self-preservation. America became increasingly necessary if the threat of nazism was to be withstood, and withstanding it meant life or death for the left much more than for the right. Were this element not strongly there I do not think it would be possible to explain the much greater degree of British interest in the Roosevelt of the second term than of the first term, even though the first was domestically so obviously the more successful. But there was an ideological content as well. And the awakening of interest in Rooseveltian politics extended not only to the President himself, but to the whole American system.

There had been American heroes in British eyes before. At the time not perhaps George Washington, but Abraham Lincoln certainly, although he was viewed by many in London rather as a sort of Che Guevara of the nineteenth century. And no man could have been revered as was Woodrow Wilson when he arrived in Europe at the end of 1918. There may have been a touch of irony in J. M. Keynes's writing of this occasion, but even so he used words which could not have been used of any other President without making irony descend into farce:

> When President Wilson left Washington, he enjoyed a prestige and moral influence throughout the world unequalled in history. His bold and measured words carried to the peoples of Europe above and beyond the voices of their own politicians. . . . Never had a philosopher held such weapons wherewith to bind the princes of the world. How the crowds of the European capitals pressed about the President! With what curiosity, anxiety and hope we sought a glimpse of the features and bearing of the man of destiny who,

coming from the West, was to bring healing to the wounds of the ancient parent of his civilisation and lay for us the foundations of the future!*

But Wilson was a knight on his own. His position was in a way much more individual and therefore less sustainable than that of Roosevelt. Bryan, Lansing, Josephus Daniels, even Colonel House, did not mean a great deal in Europe. And American politics were still regarded by many otherwise well-informed people as not worthy of serious study, a mixture of the squalid and the comic. Wilson arose for a brief period like a saint who had been mysteriously wafted up out of the poker rooms. Then he disappeared almost in a puff of smoke. Teapot Dome replaced the moral imperatives of the philosopher king, and Europe felt it had been right after all in its detached and superior view of American politics.

The Roosevelt impact was quite different. Even abroad he was never regarded as an ethereal saint, detached from the hard dealing of politics. As a result when he became a semihero, and for much longer than Wilson became a hero, he changed the whole European attitude to American politics. Nineteen thirty-six was the last presidential election which ap-

* J. M. Keynes, *The Economic Consequences of the Peace, The Collected Writings of J. M. Keynes* (London: Macmillan, 1971), p. 26.

peared to the outside world as a lot of Tammany braves dancing rather incomprehensibly but highly successfully round the wigwam. Thereafter the process gathered pace by which political scientists and television commentators from Oxford to Osaka rapidly became great experts on the psephological history of Indiana, and by which too it became extremely unfashionable not to know exactly why the Mississippi delegation might or might not be seated at a particular Democratic convention.

But Roosevelt's impact was not of course only on the left-centre. As war first drew nearer and then broke out in Europe, the need for America became greater than ever. Neville Chamberlain, stubborn in this as in so much else, remained rooted in his distrust of the President. But nearly everybody else in Britain was prepared to take a very different view. King George VI paid a notably successful visit to Washington and Hyde Park in July 1939, when the President and the King established a close and continuing relationship. FDR always had a curiously unpatrician weakness for royalty. And the King much liked being talked to more seriously about international affairs than was the habit of his ministers. As a result I think this was one of the very rare occasions when a constitutional monarch, probably by accident, played a significant part in the development of an alliance—more significant indeed than the much more publicized role alleged to have been played by King Edward VII in the creation of the *Entente Cordiale* in 1904. An odd result of the Washington and Hyde Park visit, contrary to widespread impressions, was that for the first two years of the European War, Roosevelt knew King George VI much better than he knew Churchill, and that when as Prime Minister Churchill went to the Atlantic Charter Conference in the summer of 1941, he bore with him a letter of commendation from his sovereign to FDR.

Thereafter, of course, the Roosevelt-Churchill relationship became much closer than that between King and President. There is clearly room for considerable doubt about Roosevelt's performance as a strategist and a war leader. What there is no doubt about is his acceptance by the British Prime Minister, by all but one of the other Allied governments, and even for a time by Stalin, as the captain of the West. The greatest feat of self-discipline ever exercised by Churchill in a long and not notably self-disciplined life was his determination never to quarrel with Roosevelt: argue, yes; but quarrel, no. He even put up without complaint with the White House food and the White House drink of those days—once over a stay of no less than three weeks—which he would have done in no other house in the world. It must have been a very even balance as to whether Eleanor Roosevelt found him a more trying guest, or he found her a more trying hostess.

The only Allied leader who did not accept this degree of self-discipline was De Gaulle. This was partly due to temperament, but it was also partly due to the fact that he, unlike Churchill or even Stalin, was not fighting for the preservation of his country. For France that possibility had already gone. De Gaulle was fighting for glory or honour, objectives which by their very nature invite a greater rashness of approach.

It would nevertheless be wrong to see the British wartime attitude to America as determined solely, or even principally, by a lively sense of material self-interest. There was a strong emotional response, such as is not normally evoked by those who give to those who think they ought to receive. The emissaries from America, Hopkins Winant, Harriman, Eisenhower, Willkie, were all accorded a spontaneous and not merely a self-interested respect. They came, if not like gods, at least like gladiators out of the West. The points of the compass indeed began to assume a more than geographical or mathematical significance. Of all Churchill's memorable speeches in 1940 and 1941 few touched the emotions of Britain more than his inspired quotation—who was the lucky private secretary who discovered it?—of Arthur Hugh Clough, a half-forgotten mid-nineteenth-century poet:

And not through eastern windows only
When daylight comes, comes in the light,
In front the sun climbs slow, how slowly,
But westward, look, the land is bright.

There were of course strains between America and her allies during the war. There was trouble over the early working out of the detailed arrangements for Lend-Lease; over British dollar balances in late 1943; over India throughout. But on the whole I think what is remarkable is that they were not greater. Immediately after the war was a more difficult period. Yalta sowed some suspicion in Western Europe, although I have always believed that the extent of this can be exaggerated. It was not only the White House which had illusions about relations of easy trust with the Russians after the war. But there were other factors as well. There was the inevitable sag of solidarity after the extended tension of the war years. The great figures of the wartime partnership were either dead or out of power. President Truman came to office as the least internationally known chief executive of the past forty years. In addition there was considerable moral unease (accompanied probably in the British case by relief that we did not have to take the decision) about the Hiroshima and Nagasaki bombs. There was also resentment at the abrupt termination of Lend-Lease, and a feeling throughout the ensuing months that rapid American demobilisation and dismantling of the wartime economy might presage a return to post-1919 conditions.

Nineteen forty-six was the trough year. Britain, under a new Labour Government and ground by an austerity harsher in some ways than that which had prevailed during the war, was at that stage getting on much worse with the Soviet Union than was the United States. So far from left speaking sympathetically to left, one of Labour's hopes in the 1945 election, the first brunt of the Soviet pressure was borne by the British Labour Government. Ernest Bevin, the new Foreign Secretary, was dominated by the fear that, even if there was not a Soviet-American deal over his head, the Americans would at best go home and leave a weakened Britain vainly trying to organise war-destroyed and economically prostrate countries in Western Europe against Soviet aggression. The main aim of his policy was to secure a continuing United States commitment—political, military, and economic —in Europe.

His determination was by no means the only factor, of course. But his aim was overwhelmingly fulfilled. The tentative withdrawal of 1945–46 presaged not a return to the twenties but the floodtide of commitment represented by the Marshall Plan in 1947 and the formation of NATO in 1949. Within three years of taking office, President Truman became, in policy if not in manner, the most determinedly internationally minded of all American Presidents. From the acceptance of the Greek and Turkish commitment in early 1947, he never recoiled from any necessary foreign policy decision. And America, subsequently bitterly attacked by the extreme left for its interfering capitalist hegemony in Europe and elsewhere, had in fact responded to a most urgent request from a British Labour Foreign Secretary whose roots were deeper in the working-class movement than any other world statesman of the past generation.

The heyday of this period of American commitment was the late forties and very early fifties. The alliance was fresh; the Communist challenge was clear from Berlin to Korea; Europe was only tottering very unsteadily to its feet; gratitude for the Marshall Plan was actual. There was occasional disquiet about American military discretion, mainly caused by General MacArthur's not always authorised activity, but Washington's involvement and leadership was accepted with a great deal of enthusiasm and very little question. It may have been helped by the fact that there were left-of-centre governments in both the United States and Britain. It was not a question of ideological affinity between the two, but that, if the job had to be done, governments of such orientation could best form an acceptable military alliance against Communism.

In the next decade the position was different. There was a swing to the right throughout most of the developed world. Eight years of Republican administration began in the United States and thirteen years of Conservative government in Britain. In Germany, where the government had hardly counted during the previous period, Adenauer became and remained a dominant figure. At the same time the Soviet threat, while still immanent, became a little less obvious. There was no series of events quite so frighteningly frequent as Czechoslovakia in 1947, Berlin in 1948, and Korea in 1950. The thirty-fourth President of the United States was better qualified by his experience and character to preside benignly over an established alliance than any other occupant of the White House. He did so. In retrospect his judgements look calm and his detached captaincy confidence-giving. In retrospect at least, inactivity has a good deal to be said for it. Of course he left a lot to his Secretary of State. Dulles was informed, devoted, indefatigable. But it would be idle to pretend that he was very popular with most of America's allies, Germany apart. "Foster will fly over and see you for a talk next week," which was the recurrent end to so many of Eisenhower's messages to Macmillan and others, aroused a greater sense of inevitability than of enthusiasm.

At the same time the American recession of the late fifties had some direct adverse effect upon the economies of the rest of the world, as well as upon confidence in the continuing competitive performance of the United States vis à vis the Soviet Union. In 1960 what could fairly be said was that the fifties had at least been survived without disaster; that American leadership was intact; but that it carried with it no great sense of dynamism and enthusiasm.

In consequence, the change of administration in 1961 and the change of generation which went with it were generally welcomed both by America's allies and by the Third World. West Germany then, in sharp contrast with today, was the country most firmly rooted in the rigidities of the early Cold War, and as a result Bonn was probably the only NATO capital where this friendly attitude was not found. In the Third World there were no doubt also a few exceptions. The Kennedy administration got off to a bad start with the Bay of Pigs, but it had a momentum which enabled it to take this almost on the run. And just as the last years of Eisenhower had been weakened by a poor economic performance, so the first years of Kennedy were strengthened by a gradual but sustained economic pickup. The world looked to Washington as never before, not even at the height of the Allied war effort, not even at the peak of Eisenhower's senior statesmanship. And Washington, even before the diplomatic triumph of Cuba II, was able to obliterate the ignominy of the Bay of Pigs, and flashed back to the waiting world a response indicating that the leadership role was willingly accepted.

Perhaps indeed it was too willingly accepted, for although the 1961 Inaugural Address struck a note that was to many ears greatly preferable to recent sounds which have come from Washington, it cannot now be regarded as prescient of the problems which perplexed America in her world role as the decade wore on. "Pay any price, bear any burden, meet any hardship, support any friend, oppose any foe" are resonant words. But the feeling of limitless resource and the willingness to accept limitless commitment which lay behind them may, although I say it with reluctance, have helped to create some of the problems which now confront America. Yet the immediate response and the immediate prospect were glorious ones. Writing in 1971 in a biographical essay on Robert Kennedy I sought to describe his brother's Washington of the fall of 1963 as it struck a sympathetic but detached British observer:

> The benevolent sun of the Indian summer shone on Kennedy Washington, and there was little reason to think it would not do so for at least five years to come. The city was the capital of the world in a way that it had never been before. Cuba had been a triumph for cool liberalism.

There were only about 10,000 United States troops in Vietnam. The economy was expanding without inflation. The Negro problem looked menacing, but no more so than many other problems which America had faced and overcome in the past. The country was confident and glittering. Robert Kennedy still had a brother to serve. It was six weeks before Dallas.*

This now sounds a terribly long time ago.

In my third lecture, having endeavoured to deal with Britain and Europe in my second, I will try to discuss why so much has changed in the eight years and to look to the prospect for the future.

* *The Times,* February 9, 1971.

2 BRITAIN'S CHANGING PERSPECTIVE: 1945–1971

Britain always has been primarily a European rather than an imperial power. There is one school of thought that sees us as having started in Europe and being now back on our paternal doorstep again, but after an imperial excursion lasting for most of the past three centuries. In fact we have never been away from Europe. Even at the height of our world dominion a great part of our endeavours and interests and conflicts were bound up with Europe and not with our transoceanic empire. Our culture was strongly European, and so to a large extent were the everyday details of life. Most of our diplomatic effort was devoted to trying to maintain our interests amongst European dangers, and when these peaceful efforts failed it was European wars which engaged our full national effort, inflicted major national damage, and burned themselves into our popular consciousness. It is Blenheim, Waterloo, and the Somme which are the great remembered battles of British history, not Plassy or Omdurman or even Yorktown. Nor is this fact to be attributed solely to a desire to remember victories and forget defeats: we won two, and only two, in each category.

At times we thought we could detach ourselves, but it never worked. The phrase "splendid isolation" was first used in 1896. Within eighteen years we were more deeply and disagreeably involved in Europe than at any time before or since. Our chances of keeping ourselves (and everybody else) out of the mud of Flanders might have been greater if we had attempted to be less detached. And in the last decades of empire we were still, paradoxically, engaged in the pursuit of a more exclusively European foreign policy than in the present world of the superpowers. Anthony Eden, the most vigorous (partly because the youngest) of prewar Foreign Secretaries, travelled endlessly about Europe. But his world was bounded by Lisbon to the west, Rome to the south, and Prague or at furthest Bucharest to the east. Once, venturesomely, he went to Moscow. But never once during his prewar period of office did he penetrate to Washington. Never once did he meet Roosevelt. The centre of his world and that of his immediate predecessors and successors was the European orientated Foreign Office. Their most frequent journey was by the Golden Arrow train and boat service to Paris. The quintessential background sound to their diplomacy was, as evocatively described by Harold Nicolson, the crunch of the wheels of English Rolls-Royces drawing up on the carefully swept gravel in front of the Quai d'Orsay. Sometimes a Swiss or Italian lake was the centre of the scene, but never Delhi or Canberra or even, until after the outbreak of war, the White House or the State Department.

It is therefore a myth that Britain returned to involvement with Europe only when its imperial days were over. The involvement was always both close and inevitable, in the sense that we were deeply concerned with, and affected by, what happened on the Continent, and particularly in the western part of it.

For the last fifty years or so, however, much the same, although obviously with somewhat different emphasis, could be said of the United States. The attempts of the United States to keep out, its reluctance (in the earlier days) to make commitments, its ability to survive on its own, were always stronger than ours. Yet in fact the result in 1917, in 1941, in 1949 (with the establishment of NATO), as we have seen in the first lecture, was always the same—both involvement and commitment.

The European political debate in Britain over the past twenty-five years has at last been about whether our relations with the countries of the Continent should be more akin to America's with continental European countries or to their own with each other. The attitude of both the Attlee Government and the postwar Churchill Government, which between them spanned the crucial decade from 1945–55, was firmly in favour of an American-style relationship. Ernest Bevin, Foreign Secretary in the Attlee Government, was a key architect of NATO, but kept Britain out of the European Coal and Steel Community. Eden, again Foreign Secretary in the second Churchill Government, which was formed in 1951, committed British troops to Germany for the rest of the century but tried to encourage the creation of a European army without British participation and tragically declined to be represented at the Messina Conference which led directly to the Treaty of Rome. These were the days, much more than in the twenties and thirties, when we saw ourselves at the meeting point of three circles: the Commonwealth, the North Atlantic, and the European.

This view of ourselves was fortified on the surface, although in reality undermined, by the position in which Britain emerged from World War II. The inheritance which Churchill bestowed on the British people in 1945 was at once glorious and thoroughly unsatisfactory. The facade of our family mansion was as splendid as it had ever been. The art treasures were still mostly in place. But the foundations were shaky, and the income attenuated. Our future was less clearly charted than that of any of the other major countries. The United States and the Soviet Union emerged with their roles as superpowers firmly underpinned, at least for a generation. Germany, Italy, and Japan had all suffered the harsh experience of defeat; France that of occupation. Their régimes had to be constructed almost afresh. We were subject to no such brutal adjustment. But our power, so far from being built up by the war like that of America and Russia, had in fact been substantially diminished.

It took Britain some time to realise this. She did not attempt to cling to direct colonial power. Both in Asia in the forties and Africa in the fifties and early sixties Britain accepted and even forced the pace to independence. She withdrew, inevitably, occasionally jaggedly, but on the whole with good grace, from what might be described as the more selfish part of her world role. But from the more unselfish part there was for a long time no such withdrawal. Britain continued to believe that it was her duty to police large parts of the world, to defend her former dependencies, and to maintain a network of military commitments which, in extent if not in intensity, was barely approached by the superpowers, let alone by her power equals. In this way, not for unworthy motives, she tried to cling to a precarious position as the third of the great powers.

So long as this was so we remained wedded to the "American" as opposed to the "European" approach to our relations with Europe. But gradually the attempt to maintain the third great power role became increasingly unconvincing. Economically we were not in the same league as the superpowers, and the attempt to pretend that militarily we were so produced twenty years of severe overstrain which still further exacerbated our economic weakness.

Over the same period we had to rethink our relationship with the Commonwealth. The Commonwealth exists because of the accident that all its members were until fairly recently under British rule. It has the advantage of bringing together in loose and informal but occasionally intimate association, countries almost as disparate as possible from each other in race, religion, and stages of economic or social development. It is a club which imposes few obligations and is not greatly used by the members, but which has the nearly unique distinction for a club of widening rather than narrowing the horizons of those who belong. At the same time it has the disadvantage of an almost complete lack of political or economic coherence. Try to give it this and it will almost certainly break in your hands. Neither the old, white Commonwealth, with the possible exception of the remote and overdependent New Zealand, nor the newer, coloured Commonwealth countries, most of whom have too recently achieved independence to have any wish for an early merging of their sovereignty, least of all under the leadership of the principal ex-colonial power, want any approach to a tight union. Whatever its other virtues, and they are substantial, the Commonwealth has not for some time past provided Britain with any basis for a special and satisfactory role in the world. Understandably, however, in view of our past and the superficial nexus of a strong Commonwealth which persisted in London, many were slow to recognise this.

Equally the idea of the "special relationship" in any exclusive sense between the United States and Britain has not prospered over the past ten years, both because of its inherently unequal nature and because of a certain lack of enthusiasm, for exclusivity at any rate, on both sides of the Atlantic. Nor did attempts to give it a slightly wider and more institutional framework, under the guise of the North Atlantic Free Trade Area, prove any more successful. They simply languished for lack of interest.

Hesitantly and unevenly a shift from the semidetached view of Britain's relationship with Europe which prevailed up to 1955 and beyond has been taking place during the past fifteen years. A curious and significant but confused role in this process was played by the ill-fated Suez campaign of 1956. It was Britain's last aggressive colonial war, the final station on a long line. It was carried out with very doubtful military competence, was deeply divisive at home, and aroused such hostile attitude and pressure abroad, not least in Washington, that it was bound to end in failure. Its one advantage was that it was over very quickly. The Prime Minister of the day, Sir Anthony Eden, destroyed himself both in politics and in health by his misjudgement; but happily he did not destroy many others as well. The second-in-command of his Government, Harold Macmillan, whose policy was harshly described as one of "first in, first out," suffered not destruction but almost immediate entry upon the second longest British premiership of this century.

It might have been expected that this abrupt and obvious failure would have turned Britain sharply away from her world role and towards Europe. It was more complicated than this, however. Suez was an Anglo-French failure, but both the governments and the peoples of the two countries reacted very differently to their humiliation. The British, chastened and a little guilty, drew the conclusion that, tiresomely admonitory and disloyal though some thought Mr. Dulles and even President Eisenhower to have been, the main lesson to be drawn was that no more enterprises were to be attempted without the assured support of Britain's principal ally. Hilaire Belloc's "Keep ahold of nurse, for fear of finding something worse," became for most of the next decade Britain's motto for dealing with Washington. In the earlier part of the decade there was even some attempt at a late flowering of the old special relationship. But by the end of the period "nurse" had become both too preoccupied and too bespattered by the dirt of Vietnam to perform fully her role of giving starched reassurance.

In France the reaction to Suez was quite different. There was less guilt and more anger. The lesson there learnt was never to trust the Americans and probably not the British either. When De Gaulle came to power eighteen months later this turned itself into an intransigent pursuit of French independence with the Anglo-Saxons kept as much as possible at arm's length. Suez therefore both turned the British away from the remnants of her imperial tradition and divided her deeply from France. It influenced but did not make easier her development towards a European orientation.

Nevertheless Governments from both parties, first in 1961 and then in 1967, made application to join the European Economic Community. Because of the efflux of time, if for no other reason, the degree of European commitment was probably greater on the latter occasion. There would have been no Nassau Agreement —itself an obvious throwback to the pre-1955 position—to get in the way of any post-1967 negotiations. But then, on this second occasion there were no negotiations. The French veto was applied even more firmly and at an earlier stage.

Since then there have been great changes both in the Six and in England. The veto has disappeared. For the first time it has been possible to bring the negotiations to a conclusion. There has since been some disappointment in the Community about the reaction of British public opinion. But this must be seen in the context of two vetoes, which necessarily produced some disenchantment. A double rejection of overtures, particularly when spread over nearly ten years, is likely in any circumstances to result in a considerable cooling of ardour. There has also been a British fear of the unknown, accentuated by the fact that we have in the past year experienced both unemployment and price rises on a scale unknown since the war. These almost inevitably lead to a somewhat cautious mood, particularly amongst those with the weakest defenses against these twin problems, and particularly too when entry involves additional price increases and the prospect of more rapid industrial changes. But there was nothing indecisive about the vital parliamentary vote on October 28, 1971. The vote was probably the most dramatic and significant since May 1940. The majority was bigger than expected. It was cross-party, which is unusual in Britain. And it is my own view that a majority of public opinion will fairly rapidly accept what has been decided.

I therefore now propose to turn to some of the effects which I believe will follow from British entry into the European Economic Community. It has become something of a commonplace to say that the case for entry is political more than economic. I share this view, although, despite the general movement the other way, I have myself come to think the economic case still stronger now than I believed it to be a few years ago. But I also think it important to define what is meant by *political* in this context. It does not mean either that British entry will produce an automatic harmonization of, say, our foreign policy with that of the Six, even assuming that there were quickly to be a common foreign policy existing there with which to harmonize, or that we will be immediately participating in a political community complete with a full-scale set of political institutions. Desirable developments along both these lines may well follow in due course, and I believe that our membership should assist with both. In particular we should have a substantial and special contribution to make to the gradual development of political institutions, which will be necessary if there is to be effective decision making without the disadvantages of a bureaucracy which is on the whole benevolent but not at present very effectively controlled. In due course this will involve direct elections to the European Parliament. It is difficult today to imagine a fully effective democratic assembly without such elections, even though the United States Senate survived without them until 1913. But I would not force the pace. I would like to see direct elections when—and not before—they would be likely to attract as high a poll as is normal in national elections.

The principal political case for membership from the British point of view, as indeed from that of any other candidate or existing member, is much wider and less institutional than this. Principally it is that it will substantially enlarge our ability to influence our own destiny. The easiest and most pointless of national exercises today is that of clinging portentously to the shadow of sovereignty while its substance is allowed to fly quietly out of the window. To pretend to a sovereignty which has ceased to be effective is in fact to restrict and not to preserve national freedom. Defence is the most obvious but by no means the only example. For almost any country, certainly for any power of the second rank, to attempt to provide exclusively for its own defence today would mean either that it was dependent on the whims of its neighbours to attack or defend it as they chose, or that it accepted a crippling (and still probably ineffective) burden which in turn greatly reduced its freedom to do other things. Participation in a mutual defence arrangement, even with tight guarantees and a high degree of military integration, is thus likely to increase rather than diminish a country's ability to develop as it wishes.

Equally, in the economic field, to be shut out of the main groups which determine the world's economic climate does not mean exemption from the influence of that climate, but merely a loss of influence in determining it and less strength with which to withstand its rigours. I well recall special meetings of the Group of Ten—the principal rich, monetary powers of the world—when I was Chancellor of the Exchequer, and when, I hope not entirely as a result, sterling was under fairly constant pressure. There were two of them in my time—one in Stockholm and one in Bonn—but they each took roughly the same form. We assembled in plenary session. All the ten participating Finance Ministers made opening statements of position. But before decisions could begin to be taken the Ministers of the Six (to be exact the five who were present, for Luxembourg is represented by Belgium) then said that they wished to meet together and see if they could report a joint view to us. These adjournments for the Six to meet were often very long; one of them lasted for no less than ten hours. During these long intervals I passed a good deal of time chatting and having meals with the United States Secretary of the Treasury. That was for me at least, very agreeable, but at the same time not from my point of view wholly satisfactory, for in those days there was a big difference between the United States Secretary and me. The Secretary, like me, was a little impatient at the delay, but not worried, because he then thought that he could live with whatever decision emerged from the Six. I was by no means so sure that I could do so. I did not enjoy being shut out from a decision-making process which could be crucial to the future of Britain. And indeed such are the increasing limitations to sovereignty that the position of the United States Secretary of the Treasury may soon—if not already—be approximating to that in which I found myself three or four years ago.

Economic influence in turn greatly affects political influence. To attempt military tasks beyond a nation's real economic capacity, with the almost inevitable consequence of reducing that economic capacity still further, is a certain recipe for producing a minimum of influence for a maximum of effort. For any medium-rank power today a willingness to pool sovereignty is an essential prerequisite for both influence and, in a paradoxical but real sense, national freedom. Nor, let me add in passing, although this really belongs more to the third lecture, am I convinced that the division between medium- and first-rank powers is nearly as sharp and clear as appeared to be the case as recently as five years ago.

The next point is that the accession of Britain and the other candidate countries will, I believe, have a liberating effect upon the existing European Community itself. The two vetoes which were applied to Britain's application inevitably devalued the force of the European idea and caused a debilitating ideological split within the Europe of the Six. The visions of the future which emanated from men like Robert Schuman and Jean Monnet and the inspiration which seized those who met at the proselytizing Hague Conference twenty-four years ago were not related solely to the arrangements between an exclusive group of powers. They offered a new way of learning from the bitterness and destruction of the war years, a new way of transcending the restrictions of national sovereignty. But once these objectives had been given, they could not be limited just to six countries without undermining their own basis. It was not possible convincingly to say that national sovereignty was outdated, yet to refuse to let more than a limited number of countries escape from its confines. It could not be claimed that Europe can solve its own problems only on a European basis and yet insist that European countries anxious to join should not be allowed to make a full contribution.

This was a major weakness of the Community from 1963 to 1969. And it remained one until the question of the candidate members was settled. It was not a problem which would just go away from the door of the Six. It set a limit to what De Gaulle could command. He could tell Britain that it ought to be nearer to Cape Cod than to Cap Gris-Nez, but he could not convince the other five, nor even most Frenchmen, that this was really so. One of the contributions which British entry can therefore make to the future development of the Six is the negative but important one of settling this divisive issue which, for the past nine years, has done so much to tarnish the image and weaken the momentum of the Community.

But it is not the only contribution. There are at least three further ways in which British entry should influence the development of the Community. First, it can help to ensure that it is outward-looking and Atlantic orientated. This does not mean that without British membership the Community would be a tightly knit, inward-looking group interested only in its own European back-garden. For the British to believe this would be intolerably pharisaical. France has an outstandingly good record on the quantity of its overseas aid, even if this aid is very specifically directed to the Francophone countries. Germany also has a very good aid record. She has also done far more than Britain to open up relations with Eastern Europe. In addition, negatively but importantly, Germany and Italy need, and feel they need, the American defence commitment quite as much as Britain does.

Nevertheless it is inevitably the case, first, that Britain has a wider recent experience and a closer contact with the needs of the broad spectrum of developing countries throughout both Asia and Africa, including India, the crucial problem country, than any of the existing members of the European Community. In relations with the Third World this can be of great importance, and in particular it makes us more likely to encourage one desirable and necessary development—the channelling of a high and increasing proportion of aid through international agencies.

Second, reasons of history and geography unite in ensuring that Britain would always want to see a European Community of which it was a member joined by close and friendly links with the United States. There are few in Britain who would want to abolish the English Channel at the price of making the Atlantic into an unbridgeable chasm. Our role here requires careful definition. If we see it as being that of standing half outside Europe and trying from a mid-Atlantic position—as a sort of enlarged Iceland—to act as an intermediary between Europe and the United States, I think we would make General De Gaulle not turn but smile in his grave, and would end ourselves in rather foolish failure. But if we see our role as being fully part of Europe, but a part which, because of our tradition and outlook, is likely always to use its influence so as to make European unity fully compatible with close links across the Atlantic, we will better serve both our own needs and those of the Atlantic Community as a whole. Furthermore, the best basis for a continuing close North Atlantic relationship is the nearest possible approach to equality between the assembled European partners on the one side and the United States on the other, a closer approach to equality than has been possible during the life of the alliance so far. A Europe of which Britain is part is much more likely, for simple reasons of population, as well as military and economic power, to be able to achieve such a close approach to equality than is one from which Britain is excluded. Such an approach to equality is at least as much in the interests of the United States as it is in that of the European countries. This was true even while the United States was bearing its massive responsibilities with equanimity. It is still more true today, when the equanimity is a little strained.

It follows from the preceding analysis that the issues at stake in the question of our entry are very big ones for Britain, for the existing Community, and to a lesser although still substantial extent for much of the rest of the world. For the Community enlargement is essential to achieve its full strength and be faithful to its original European idealism. For Britain the central point is our national self-confidence. It has been battered a good deal in the past twenty-five years. The cautious, insular, unadventurous, misguided view is for Britain to try to protect itself from further bruises by turning in upon itself and pretending that by so doing we are saving our greatness. In fact we should be doing nothing of the sort. In doing so we should merely be saying that the world had got too much for us. Outside the Community we could of course survive, and no doubt achieve modest, although in my view needlessly modest, increases in prosperity. But we would find it increasingly difficult for our role in world affairs to be a significant one. Inside we could still aspire to a considerable role of benevolent influence, an influence the stronger for being based upon a realistic and not an exaggerated and therefore self-defeating view of our economic, military, and monetary strength.

3 THE FUTURE INTERNATIONAL ROLE OF THE UNITED STATES

One of my difficulties in considering the future is that in my last two lectures I got Britain and the mainland of Western Europe to 1971, but left the United States suspended in 1963. This was due to no intentional discrimination. I merely found American history, because less familiar to me, more interesting than European, and found 1963 a more natural breaking point on this side of the Atlantic than on my own. But it means that I have to begin looking at the future with a brief United States retrospect. In a way, of course, this is a relief. It is much easier to describe the past than to predict the future. But this particular segment of the American past is a very difficult one to describe, especially for someone who was for much of the time a member of a closely allied government.

The presidency of Lyndon B. Johnson was, and is likely to remain, one of the most elusive to evaluate. It began in tragedy and five years later it ended in tragedy of a different sort. In the earlier part of the quinquennium a great deal was accomplished in the United States. The "we shall overcome" speech at Philadelphia in 1964 stirred hearts all over the world—and action at home as well—as much as any of the most remembered orations of American history. Furthermore, the seeds of the disaster which destroyed Lyndon Johnson's presidency as well as a great deal else had clearly been sown before his accession to power, although the failure to contain the growth was very much his own. At the same time there is an element of bathos about the strong exercise of imperial power from Washington such a short time before the semicollapse of much of its basis. A fairly strict alliance discipline was attempted. It was not only congressional arms that were twisted.

I recall how in early 1968 the British Government decided, necessarily but belatedly in my view, that we were going to fix an earlier terminal date for our military withdrawal from the Far East. Our Foreign Secretary went to Washington with advance warning of the news and reported that our plans were unsympathetically received. We were lectured about being too concerned with our economy, which had been in heavy and dangerous balance of payments deficit for years, and too little with our world policing role. We put up with the lecture and stuck to our plan. After it had been announced, the Prime Minister went in turn to Washington. Apart from a doubtfully tactful inclusion of "The Road to Mandalay" in the programme for a White House musical evening, he was magnanimously forgiven. But the mood was one of "poor old Britain." So badly did we manage our economy that we could not properly afford our proper role of being an auxiliary world power.

There is a certain irony now in looking back at this pattern of events. It was hardly contemplated then that the United States, with an economy ten times the size of the British and a per capita wealth never previously seen in the world, would within three years be facing the British crisis, writ large, and in a still more acute form.

Yet this is almost exactly what has happened, except that, perhaps true to American traditions, it has all occurred in the United States with greater speed and greater intensity. Over twenty-five years, slightly to paraphrase Dean Acheson's famous and astringent remark, we lost or rather withdrew from an empire, and were slow to find an alternative role. Over five years the United States lost—or rather failed to win—a war, and suffered terrible divisions at home partly as a consequence. Both experiences have been somewhat destructive of national self-confidence.

In addition the United States has come abruptly up against the limitations of its financial and economic power, an experience with which we in Britain have lived uncomfortably and on the whole have adjusted to rather ineffectively since 1945. But it is American problems with which I wish to deal today, and which are in any event of somewhat greater concern to the world as a whole. It would be extremely narrow-sighted to see American dilemmas today solely in terms of failure to secure a military solution in South-East Asia, combined with an inability to find the resources both to lead the world and solve domestic problems. There are deeper moral questions at issue, touching the whole relationship of individuals to society and the whole question of material values. Yet I think it valuable, at least for ground-clearing and for illustrative purposes as well, to try to see what has happened internationally to the United States in the financial and economic field. What has happened militarily is more obvious.

At Bretton Woods twenty-seven years ago a system was set up by which the dollar became the anchor currency of the world. Other countries undertook the obligation to support their own currencies so that they did not fluctuate, except within narrow and defined points, against the dollar. At times of pressure they had to use their reserves for this purpose. The United States did not have this obligation. It had the wider one of maintaining the only currency still linked to gold and of being at least theoretically willing to pay out gold for dollars whenever other countries demanded this.

To be the reserve banker of the world was a heavy responsibility for any country to undertake. It meant that other countries could from time to time improve their competitive positions by devaluing against the dollar, as many of them did, some quite frequently, but that the United States could never do the same by devaluing against them. All that it could attempt was to persuade others to revalue. Only in a very few cases did the persuasion work. Until the present fundamental weakness of the system began urgently to show itself, in 1968–69, the score was fifty-nine devaluations to four revaluations.

It is a matter of history, however, that the United States voluntarily chose this system. If it had accepted Keynes's 1944 plan for a world clearing union, with heavy obligations upon surplus countries, it could have had *Bancor* and not the dollar as the world reserve unit. It chose otherwise. It welcomed the special position for the dollar, and it resisted too great an obligation being placed upon surplus countries. In the circumstances of the time and of the subsequent decade or so, with the apparently impregnable American competitive position and the massive trade surpluses which flowed from this, it was at least a comprehensible decision. And it must be said that it was a decision which provided the world with a system which worked, not perfectly but with a high degree of success, for nearly a generation. Never in the history of the world have trade and prosperity expanded as fast as in this period of dollar hegemony.

But foresight, as is usually the case, did not prove complete. Sterling, as the auxiliary reserve currency, was in frequent difficulty almost from the beginning. The United Kingdom's economy, in retrospect at least, was manifestly too small to support such a responsibility. The attitude of the United States to the problem was rather similar to that which I described earlier in relation to our military withdrawal from the Far East. It was at once sympathetic and admonitory. We were given a great deal of help to sustain the unsustainable, and as bits of the burden fell involuntarily from our shoulders, Washington always picked them up. But we were greatly discouraged from a drastic but necessary readjustment. We were encouraged to postpone our devaluation, which eventually came in 1967, to a later date than was sensible, on the ground that it would be the beginning of the collapse of the temple. Perhaps that was true, for soon after our belated action, the troubles of the dollar began. The 1968 Gold Crisis was the start of a series which gathered momentum until the autumn of 1969 and then paused for a year or so before working up to its culmination in the summer of 1971.

The United States should not be blamed for a fairly drastic reaction to these developments. There is no sense and little virtue in standing to attention, frozen in an immobile salute and singing patriotic songs, as the water rises to one's neck and beyond. The question is whether the reaction is a correct one. The United States is now clearly entitled to demand to be released from the special burden of acting as the pivot of the whole world monetary system. This no longer fits the facts of economic geography. The special privileges, such as they are, will of course go too. The dollar will no longer be "the imperial currency," as the French used so jealously to call it.

It can be replaced by no other national currency, nor even, I think, by that of a group of countries such as the European Community. Only a world reserve unit, growing out of Special Drawing Rights, and freed I hope of any connection with gold, which De Gaulle grandiloquently saw as "immutable, impartial, and universal" in its judgements, but which I see as restrictive and haphazard, can in the future perform the pivotal or anchor role. The dollar will have the right to fluctuate against this international standard, in accordance preferably with certain agreed rules, as much as any other currency. But within these rules it will have to support itself in world markets using its own reserves for the purpose and borrowing from the International Monetary Fund if these need to be supplemented, just as any other country. And if it wishes to effect a change in its parity this must be done by a devaluation rather than by expecting everyone else to do a series of revaluations. There is, I believe, a growing acceptance of this, although there seemed a danger in the early autumn of 1971 that, a crisis having quite reasonably, indeed inevitably, been caused by the need of the United States to escape from the strait jacket of inability to devalue, the United States government was at the same time complaining that any suggestion that it should actually do so, as opposed to everyone else's performing a covering-up operation, was a most outrageous assault upon its sovereignty.

This is not primarily a monetary or economic lecture and I do not therefore attempt to deal with all the details which will be involved in the change to a substantially modified Bretton Woods. There are considerable problems relating to the Eurodollar Market, to short-term capital flows in and out of the United States, to wider margins, to the future use of the parity adjustment process. What I am more concerned with here is the fact that much of America's longer-term political and military problems are vividly illustrated by her current monetary and trading problems—they are of course in a sense the reverse side of the same coin—and that the pull of the temptations and short-term interests on the one hand and of the duties and longer-term interests on the other illuminate many of the pressures between which she will have to make wider policy decisions in the future.

Hitherto the monetary role was one of clear leadership. It was not a question of being *primus inter pares.* It was much more comparable to a sun with its satellites, or a father—and one in a stronger patriarchal tradition than is usual today—with his children. It was a benevolently run family, but it was one in which all the main responsibilities rested upon the father. Of course if one of the children got into financial trouble he was expected to improve his performance for the future. If it was one of the junior children the instructions for improvement could be given, perhaps using the maternal influence of the International Monetary Fund, in a fairly blunt form. If it was one of the senior ones it was done, again partly through the same agency, more gently. "Reasoning together" was the accepted approach. But in either case, until the hoped-for improvement could take place, it was the father of the family—the United States—who provided most of the resources to get over the difficulties. Quite often this had to be done time and time again. It was nearly always done with exemplary patience, generosity, and even affection. Occasionally there was a little growling resentment at apparent lack of gratitude, a feeling that those who took loans from the family purse ought to show a more uncritical respect for the judgement and scale of values of the head of the family. But in general it was responsibility and family leadership exercised in an admirable and exemplary way.

At the same time it should not be pretended that there is not considerable self-satisfaction to be derived from the performance of such a role. It gives a secure feeling of position, of influence, of being needed. If suddenly that position disappears, because the resources of the head of the family have become severely strained, because some of the children, in relation to their accustomed standard of living at least, have actually become richer than the head, because a whole new pattern of relationships has to be worked out, this imposes a much greater strain than a continuance of the old, established, accustomed pattern. There is then a strong tendency for the patriarch who finds that circumstances have displaced him to say: "I did my best. It was a pretty good best. I did it for a long time. Now apparently I am no longer needed in the same way. I will retire. I will look after myself. If I cannot have the satisfaction of benevolently running the whole show, I will seek the contrary satisfaction of being a selfish old man." If the change were such that the former leader had become an old and unimportant figure, ready for the retirement home and nothing else, then such a switch of attitude would not matter much, beyond the sad fact that his recipe for self-concern would almost certainly condemn him to a miserable and cantankerous old age.

But this would be a wild caricature of what has happened to the United States in the monetary sphere, with which, largely for illustrative purposes, I am still dealing. She has not become unimportant. She is merely in the awkward process of moving from being the qualitatively different pivot of the whole to being *primus inter pares*. But however the process of adjustment is carried through, she will for a substantial time at least, remain *primus*. Her capacity to do harm, as well as good, both to herself and others, will remain immense.

Such a limited adjustment is in many ways psychologically more difficult than a more complete one. It requires far more self-discipline. If it meant a complete retirement from the centre to the remote periphery then all sort of indulgences would be in order. The dollar could be managed with the most brutal disregard for international consequences. The United States could move far in a fully protectionist direction. The damage to the rest of the world and the repercussive effect on America in these wholly imaginary circumstances would not be very great. But this is not remotely the position. America is not becoming a post-imperial Spain. Her every move will still have a greater effect on the prosperity and trading health of the whole world than those of any other three countries put together.

Decisions about such moves must be taken from a position just a little less eminent than the previous one, but in the knowledge that the consequences for good or evil are still vast. America's attitude to protection can still do more than anything else to determine whether we retain the relatively bland world trading climate which has done so much to increase prosperity both at home and elsewhere in the past twenty-five years; or whether we move back to a more narrowly restrictionist world in which the harsh, short-sighted pursuit of an immediate trading advantage will produce both long-term impoverishment and a bitterness of relations which will spill out far wider than the trade field. America's attitude to development aid can still do more than anything else to determine whether there is a future of economic hope for the poor countries, or whether the continuance and even the intensification of grinding poverty and hunger is still the only prospect for the majority of the world's inhabitants.

There is a view whose proponents would say that the longer-sighted, outward-looking, internationally responsible approach was in general valid but must be greatly modified at the present time by the pressing need of the United States to deal with its own internal problems: to improve the cities and to heal the divisions, both racial and economic, which disfigure the country. The backyard, it can be argued, now demands priority over the world outside. Some force can be allowed to the argument. No one would deny the urgency of these problems. Nor can it be disputed that America's image has been tarnished and her capacity for leadership impaired by the hardening of divisions at home and by the violence which this has in part caused.

Yet I find the conclusion unconvincing, and I find it so for this reason. It is precisely the individuals, the groups, the institutions who are most concerned about America's responsibilities abroad who are also most concerned about her internal problems. And it is also those who most advocate a selfish attitude abroad who are most selfish at home. The view that every country is an island goes in the great majority of cases with the view that every man is an island too. If a movement of opinion is created, by which great sums, for example, are saved on development aid, I do not see that movement of opinion insisting that those great sums be switched to rescuing the ghettos of the cities. I think it far more likely that they will find their way into already well-lined private pockets. The world should not and will not be impatient of increasing American concern with its own daunting domestic problems. But the solution to them will go with a generous, outward-looking, community approach which cannot easily stop short at the Statue of Liberty and the Golden Gate Bridge.

So far I have dealt mainly with the impact of recent economic developments upon the future. I have done so partly because of their inherent importance, but partly also because they are so sharply illustrative of the general problem of American adjustment to the world of the seventies and eighties, which will be still more significantly different from that of the fifties and sixties than these two decades were from each other. The political and military balance is not changing in such a clear-cut way as is the monetary balance. There is no political Bretton Woods system which has run its span and now has to be refurbished. There is no exact military equivalent to the anchor role of the dollar which can no longer be sustained. Yet the parallels are real even if not precise.

The world of well-defined confrontation, with America leading the West almost as clearly as the Soviet Union led the Eastern block, with no other major power in the picture, with the Third World an amorphous if vociferous group, is clearly breaking into a new pattern. Within NATO, the continued existence of which will in my view be necessary for a considerable time to come, the balance has changed somewhat, and will I believe do so further, partly as a result of the accession of Britain and the other candidate members to the European Economic Community. There will be a greater approach to equality on both sides of the Atlantic, an approach which will be as much in America's interests as in that of the European partners. The nuclear capacity will remain overwhelmingly American, and as a result so will the responsibility for nuclear limitation negotiations with the Soviet Union. But the balance of other forces within the alliance has tilted and will continue to tilt in a European direction. So, perhaps more significantly, will the opportunity for seeking reductions of tension and the loosening of blocs in Central Europe. A German initiative on the scale of Willy Brandt's *Ostpolitik* would have been hardly conceivable ten years ago. The possibility of such developments, on a wider scale, will be enhanced if the enlarged European Community can develop more of a political identity. And we may hope that it will be matched by some considerable loosening of Soviet control over the Eastern European countries. In any event the emergence of China, with its public abandonment of any attempt at a special relationship with the Soviet Union, clearly destroys a bipolar view of the world. In addition, the increasingly unanchored position of Japan and its rapidly growing economic power further break up the pattern by which every rich and developed non-Communist country was neatly tucked up in the Western alliance.

Elsewhere in the world there are further and growing limitations to what can be done from Washington. Just as I have long regarded it as a clear lesson of history that the British political genius, great though this may be in certain fields, does not extend to a peculiar talent for settling the affairs of Ireland, so I think it should now be accepted that the same lesson applies to the ability of the United States for settling the affairs of South-East Asia. And the United States at least has the advantage that Vietnam is in no way part of its metropolitan homeland, as is Northern Ireland of ours. Slowly, perhaps, the United States can disengage itself from its mistakes. We have to live with ours. Nor do either of us, Britain with the legacy of its imperial connections, the United States with its aid sanctions and other forms of leverage, seem to have much influence on the Indian subcontinent. I think this should be recognized by standing back a little, using our good offices through the United Nations certainly, but not considering ourselves too much as headmasters who always have to be handing out certificates for good and bad behaviour.

The general picture in the political field is therefore again one in which the United States must inevitably play a somewhat less dominant role than in the past generation. Yet here again, as in the monetary field, it is vital that the changed needs of an evolving world are not equated with rejection of America's role. The American tent will in the future not be quite so gloriously and uniquely sited on the very top of the highest hill, nor gleaming quite so conspicuously with all the insignia of the supreme and universally recognised commander-in-chief as hitherto. But it will still have a prominent and vital position for the future of the world. The act of statesmanship now required is to resist any temptation to use the inevitably slightly lowered position of the tent as an excuse for skulking within it. The contribution still to be made by the United States is immense. Speaking today thirty years and two days after Pearl Harbor, and looking back on this period of benevolent dominance, I believe that the tests of American self-confidence will be still greater, although perhaps less obvious, in the future. But they are by no means insurmountable tests. I hope that in December 2001, after another thirty years, the world will on balance have at least as good cause for gratitude and the American people for solid but not complacent satisfaction as they have in the context of today's retrospect.